PERCUSSION

AN INTRODUCTION TO MUSICAL INSTRUMENTS

By Dee Lillegard

CHILDRENS PRESS ®

CHICAGO

PHOTO CREDITS
Journalism Services:

© H. Rick Bamman—10, 12, 13, 16, 18
© Paul F. Gero—3 (right)
© Joseph Jacobson—5, 14, 21
© Mike Kidulich—17, 22
© Harvey Moshman—6
© James F. Quinn—26

Nawrocki Stock Photo:

© Michael Brohm—9, 20, 24
© Rui Coutinho—15 (top)
© Myron Davis—3 (left)
© Robert Lightfoot—11, 25, 28, 29
© Phylane Norman—4
© Ken Sexton—back cover, 8
© D. Variakojis—15 (bottom)
© Carlos Vergara—7, 23
© Jim Wright—27

The Photo Source/Three Lions—cover, 19

Art on pages 30 and 31 by Tom Dunnington

Library of Congress Cataloging-in-Publication Data

Lillegard, Dee
  Percussion.

  Summary: A brief introduction to the musical
instruments of the percussion family.
    1.   Percussion instruments—Juvenile literature.
[1.   Percussion instruments]   I.   Title.
ML3928.L53   1987   789'.01   87-18217
ISBN 0-516-02216-4

Childrens Press, Chicago
Copyright © 1987 by Regensteiner Publishing Enterprises, Inc.
All rights reserved. Published simultaneously in Canada.
Printed in the United States of America.
1 2 3 4 5 6 7 8 9 10 R 96 95 94 93 92 91 90 89 88 87

Bongo drums (left) are played with the hands. Other kinds of drums (right) are played with drumsticks.

Percussion means hitting.
Bang on a can. Bang on
a pan. That's percussion.
Pound on a drum. Tap
with your thumb. That's
percussion.

3

Snare drums (opposite page) and bass drums (above) are percussion instruments.

Here come the **percussion** instruments!

March with the big **bass drum**. *Boom-boom-boom.* The big **bass drum** makes everyone march in time. It has a deep, low sound.

Snare drums are also called side drums.

Play the little **snare drum**.
It is also called a side
drum. Drummer boys used
to play this instrument as

6

soldiers marched to war. It has a higher sound than the big bass drum. Sometimes it sounds sad.

Drummers in a military band

The kettledrum is also called a timpani.
It is played with mallets.

Play a **timpani**, or
kettledrum. Strike it with a
mallet, not just a stick. Use
a soft mallet or a hard mallet.
Different mallets make
different sounds. The

timpani is the only drum that can play notes.

If you play fast, you can play a *roll*. A quiet roll sounds like one long note. A loud roll sounds like a storm. Play the wonderful, *thunder*-ful **kettledrum**!

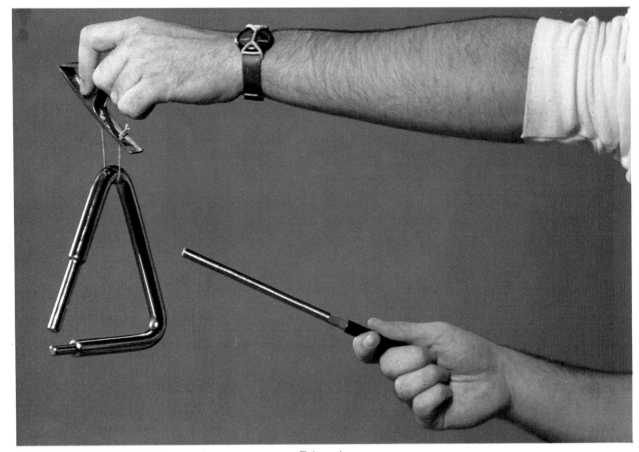

Triangle

A **triangle** is made of
metal. Strike it with a
short metal beater. It makes
a nice *ting*.

10

Cymbals look like two brass plates. You can hold them by their straps and brush them against each other. Or you can strike them with a soft or hard stick. A crash of **cymbals** will wake anyone up!

Play the **chimes**. They
are made of metal. They
sound just like bells.

Chimes

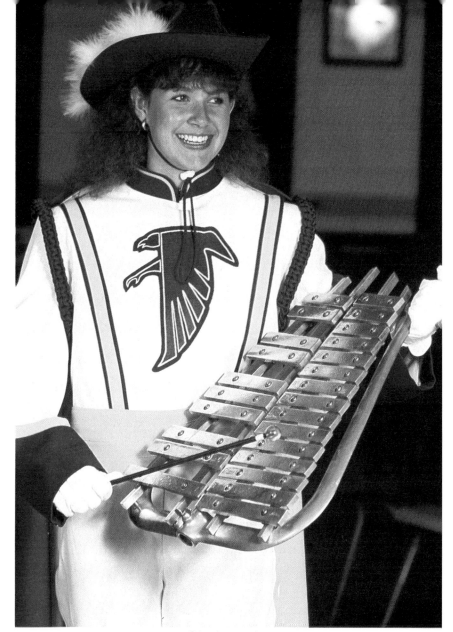

Glockenspiel

The **glockenspiel** may be
easier to play than to say.
It also sounds like bells.

This vibraphone is a special kind of xylophone.

Play the **xylophone**. Its
bars are made of wood. Strike
them with mallets. Hear the
quick, bright sound?

These musicians are playing different kinds of xylophones.

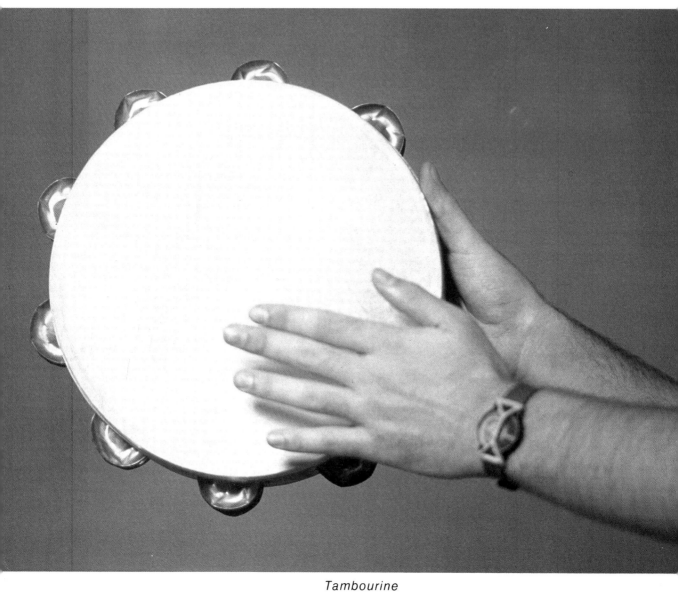

Tambourine

The **tambourine** is a small,
shallow drum. You can shake
it or strike it with your

16

hand. The little metal circles jingle. The **tambourine** is a Spanish instrument.

Chimes, tambourines, and triangles each have their own special sound.

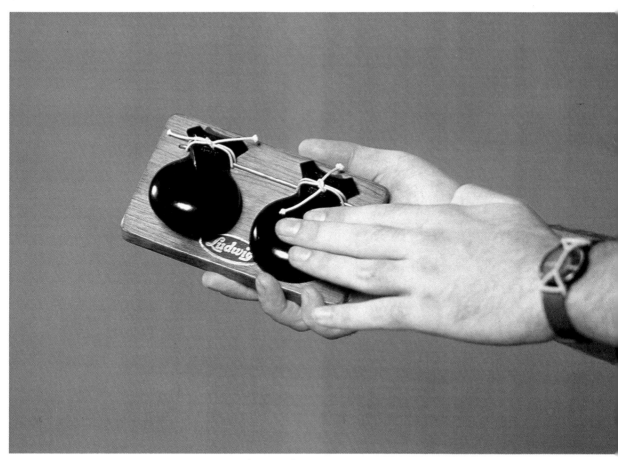

It's fun to dance to castanets.

Castanets are Spanish,
too. They are small wooden
clappers that you hold in your
hands. They *click*, *click*,
click to the rhythm of the
Spanish dancers.

18

Percussion section of an orchestra

The **percussion** part of an
orchestra is sometimes called
the *kitchen*. It has clanging,
banging, and splashing. Its

sounds add spice to the other instruments.

Almost every band or orchestra has a drummer.

This singer plays the piano.

Now play one more
percussion instrument. It is
a special one—the **piano**.

The **piano** has 88 keys. Strike some of them with your fingers. What happens?

Close-up of a piano keyboard

Hammers, covered with felt, hit the strings inside the piano.

There are strings
inside the **piano**. There are
hammers with felt tips, too.
When your fingers strike the
keys, the hammers strike the
strings.

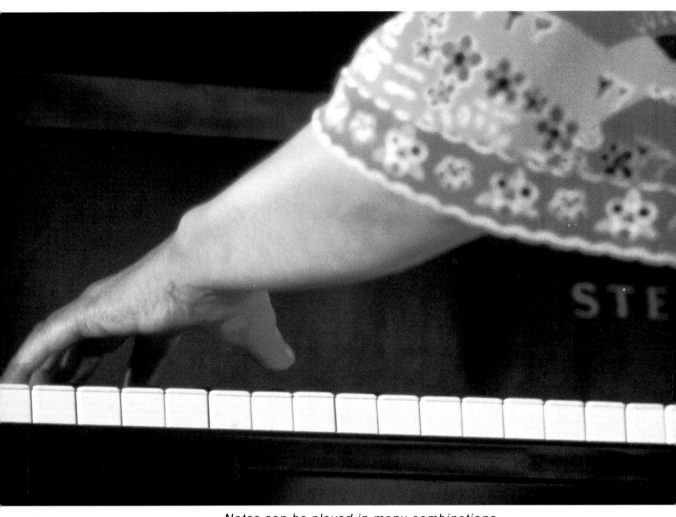
Notes can be played in many combinations on a piano.

The 88 keys make 88 different notes. These notes can be played together in many different ways. You can

Most people learn to play the piano from teachers.

play the **piano** loudly or softly. You can play slow songs or fast songs, sad songs or happy songs.

Teenagers play in a steel drum band.

Sometimes it's easy to
play a **percussion** instrument,
sometimes it's not.

Sometimes you can play a **percussion** instrument alone —especially the piano. Most of the others you will play with other instruments. **Percussion** can be fun!

𝄞 WIND INSTRUMENTS

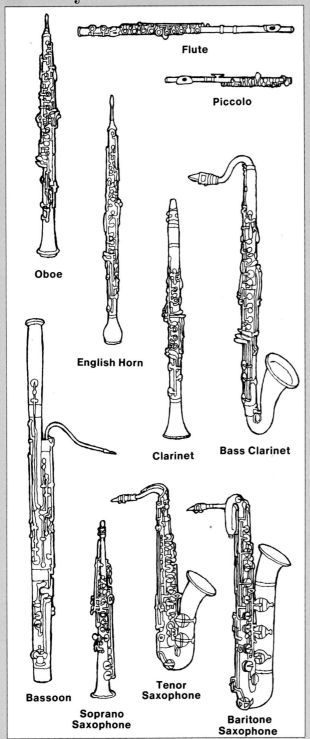

Flute

Piccolo

Oboe

English Horn

Clarinet

Bass Clarinet

Bassoon

Soprano
Saxophone

Tenor
Saxophone

Baritone
Saxophone

𝄞 PERCUSSION INSTRUMENTS

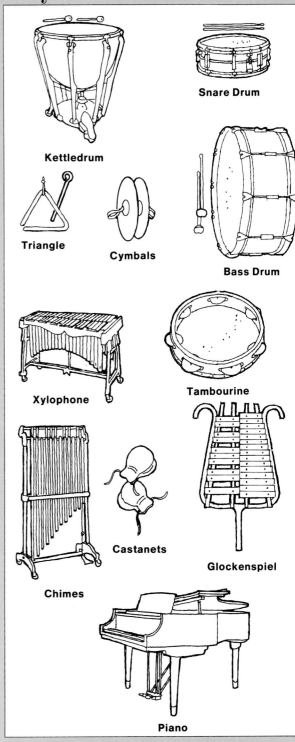

Snare Drum

Kettledrum

Triangle

Cymbals

Bass Drum

Xylophone

Tambourine

Chimes

Castanets

Glockenspiel

Piano

♪ STRINGED INSTRUMENTS

Bowed | **Plucked**

Violin

Viola

Cello

Bass

Mandolin

Guitar

Ukulele

Banjo

Harp

♪ BRASS INSTRUMENTS

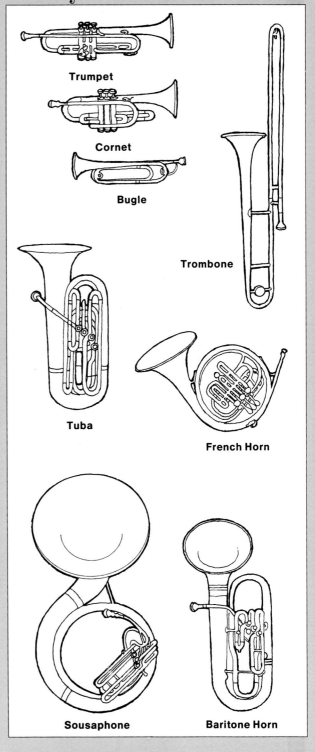

Trumpet

Cornet

Bugle

Trombone

Tuba

French Horn

Sousaphone

Baritone Horn

ABOUT THE AUTHOR

Dee Lillegard (born Deanna Quintel) is the author of over two hundred published stories, poems, and puzzles for children, plus *Word Skills*, a series of high-interest grammar worktests, and *September to September*, *Poems for All Year Round*, a teacher resource. Ms. Lillegard has also worked as a children's book editor and teaches writing for children in the San Francisco Bay Area. She is a native Californian.